A Note to Parents and Teachers

DK READERS is a compelling program for beginning readers, designed in conjunction with leading literacy experts, including Dr. Linda Gambrell, director of the Eugene T. Moore School of Education, Clemson University, and past president of the National Reading Conference.

Beautiful illustrations and superb full-color photographs combine with engaging, easy-to-read stories to offer a fresh approach to each subject in the series. Each DK READER is guaranteed to capture a child's interest while developing his or her reading skills, general knowledge, and love of reading.

The four levels of DK READERS are aimed at different reading abilities, enabling you to choose the books that are exactly right for your children:

Level 1 – Beginning to read
Level 2 – Beginning to read alone
Level 3 – Reading alone
Level 4 – Proficient readers

The "normal" age at which a child begins to read can be anywhere from three to eight years old, so these levels are only a general guideline.

No matter which level you select, you can be sure that you are helping your child learn to read, then read to learn!

LONDON, NEW YORK, MELBOURNE,
MUNICH, and DELHI

Senior Editor Beth Sutinis
Senior Art Editor Michelle Baxter
Publisher Chuck Lang
Creative Director Tina Vaughan
Production Chris Avgherinos

Reading Consultant
Linda Gambrell, Ph.D.

Produced by
Shoreline Publishing Group
Editorial Director James Buckley, Jr.
Art Director Tom Carling
Carling Design, Inc.

Produced in partnership and licensed by
Major League Baseball Properties, Inc.
Vice President of Publishing
Don Hintze

First American Edition, 2003
03 04 05 10 9 8 7 6 5 4 3 2 1

Published in the United States by DK Publishing, Inc.
375 Hudson St., New York, NY 10014

Published in Great Britain by Dorling Kindersley Limited

A catalog record is available from the Library of Congress

0-7894-9842-1 (PB)
0-7894-9843-X (HC)

Color reproduction by Colourscan, Singapore
Printed and bound in China by L Rex Printing Co., Ltd.

Photography credits:
All photos courtesy of MLB Photos and the Baseball
Hall of Fame and Library except: AP/Wide World, 30t;
Library of Congress, 10, 37.

Discover more at
www.dk.com

Contents

 **READERS**

READING
3
ALONE

MAJOR LEAGUE BASEBALL

RECORD BREAKERS

Written by Jon Scher

DK Publishing, Inc.

Pitching

Nolan with the Angels.

Can you imagine being able to throw a baseball 100 miles per hour? Nolan Ryan could do it. When he was young, Nolan threw the ball so hard he got blisters on his fingers. To make them feel better, he soaked them in pickle juice!

In 1973, while pitching for the California Angels, Nolan set a major league record with 383 strikeouts. It was the first of many records to come.

Batters were afraid of Nolan's fastball. Even he didn't always know where it was going. "It helps if the hitter thinks you're a little crazy," Nolan said.

As he got older, Nolan got better control of his pitches.

That control helped him play in the major leagues for 27 seasons. He retired in 1993 with 5,714 career strikeouts—nearly 1,600 more than any other pitcher.

Nolan had a ball with the Texas Rangers.

Kerry Wood

Whether you call it a whiff, a punchout, or a K, a strikeout thrills the crowd and sends the batter moping back to the dugout, dragging his bat behind him.

The record for most strikeouts in a nine-inning game is 20. It has only been done four times in baseball history (remember, there are just 27 outs in a nine-inning game).

Two of the three pitchers to set this mark, Kerry Wood and Roger "The Rocket" Clemens, grew up in Texas as fans of Nolan Ryan.

Pitching for the Boston Red Sox in 1986, Roger became the first to "fan" 20. He repeated his feat in 1996 for the Toronto Blue Jays.

In 1998, when he was just a rookie. Kerry Wood joined the 20-strikeout club. His uniform number, 34, is the same as Nolan's!

Mighty Arizona Diamondbacks lefthander Randy Johnson became the most recent to strike out 20 in a game. He did it in 2001.

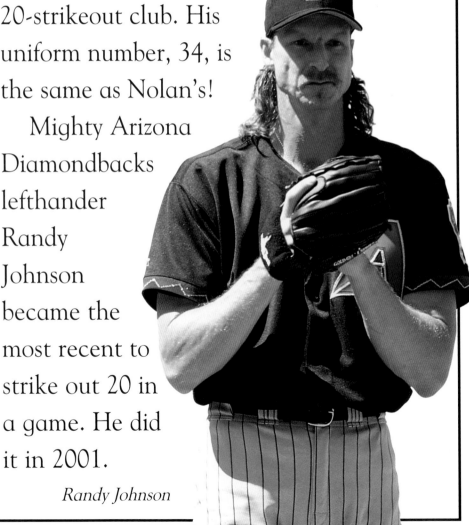

Randy Johnson

Every year, the best pitcher in each league wins the Cy Young Award. Who was Cy Young, anyway?

His real name was Denton True Young. Young Denton got his nickname after one of his pitches broke a fence and someone said it looked like a cyclone had hit it!

Hall of Famer Cy Young

Cy won 511 games in his career (1890–1911), a record that will never be broken because pitchers today don't pitch as often as they used to.

Cy didn't think much of modern teams with 10 pitchers. "Pitch 'em every three days and you'd find they'd get control and good, strong arms."

Walter Johnson of the Washington Senators was the most intimidating pitcher in the early days *Walter Johnson* of baseball. Known as "The Big Train," he set a record with 110 shutouts. His 3,509 strikeouts were the record until Nolan Ryan came along.

Rocket's record
Roger "The Rocket" Clemens of the Yankees has won the Cy Young Award a record six times in his career.

Once upon a time, baseball teams used only two starting pitchers. It was common for pitchers to win 40 or even 50 games a season. Charley "Old Hoss" Radbourn set the all-time record in 1884 with 59 wins! His arm must have been made of rubber!

Today, the best starters usually win 20 or more games a season. Only one pitcher, Denny McLain of the Detroit Tigers, has broken the 30-win barrier since 1934. Denny set the modern-day standard with 31 victories in 1968. He helped the Tigers win their first World Series since 1945. (Denny also wore a white mink coat and played the piano on TV's *The Ed Sullivan Show!*)

An old baseball card of "Old Hoss" Radbourn

Denny McLain prepares to let one fly for the Tigers.

The 1968 season was also called the Year of the Pitcher. Batting averages were the lowest they've ever been. Only one American League player, Boston's Carl Yastrzemski, hit over .300!

Yankees ace Whitey Ford

Whitey Ford of the New York Yankees won a record 10 World Series games. No pitcher was better when the title was on the line.

The Yankees won 11 American League pennants and six World Series during Whitey's career. No one has come close to his Series marks, including strikeouts (94) and consecutive scoreless innings (33 in 1960, 1961, and 1962).

"The bases could be loaded and the pennant riding on every pitch, it never bothered Whitey," said slugger Mickey Mantle.

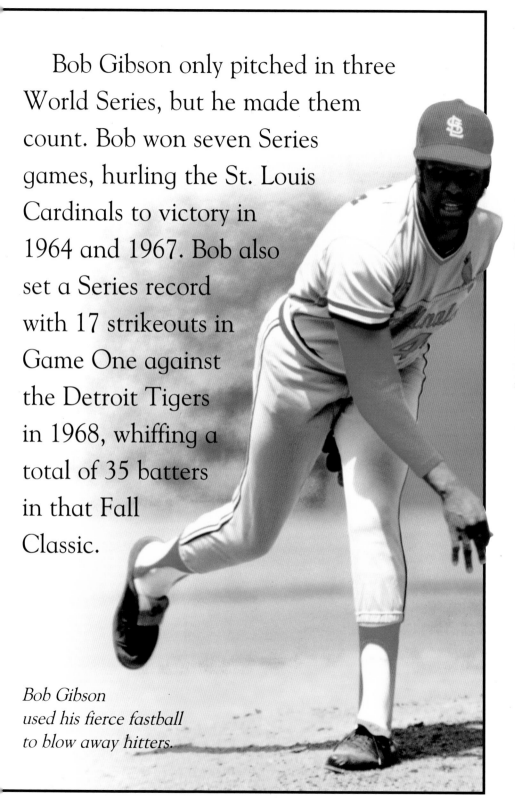

Bob Gibson only pitched in three World Series, but he made them count. Bob won seven Series games, hurling the St. Louis Cardinals to victory in 1964 and 1967. Bob also set a Series record with 17 strikeouts in Game One against the Detroit Tigers in 1968, whiffing a total of 35 batters in that Fall Classic.

Bob Gibson used his fierce fastball to blow away hitters.

Hitting

Ted Williams often said hitting a baseball is the hardest thing to do in sports. He should know—he did it better than just about anyone else.

Ted Williams

Nicknamed "The Splendid Splinter" because he was such a skinny kid, Ted was the last player to hit better than .400 for a season. In 1941, Ted hit an amazing .406 for the Boston Red Sox. In 1942, he won the A.L. Triple Crown (leading the league in average, homers, and RBI) with a .356 average, 36 homers, and 137 runs batted in. He took the Triple Crown again in 1947.

Ted missed nearly five seasons of his career to military service—he was a Marine Corps fighter pilot in World War II and the Korean War. Still, he finished his baseball career with 521 homers and a .344 average. Ted said, "A man has to have goals." His goal was to have people say, "There goes Ted Williams, the greatest hitter who ever lived."

Since Ted Williams retired, only two players have approached the .400 mark. George Brett of the Kansas City Royals hit .390 in 1980. Tony Gwynn of the San Diego Padres hit .394 in 1994.

Tony Gwynn won eight National League batting titles.

Tony was by far the best pure hitter in baseball's recent history. He retired in 2001 with a .338 lifetime average.

Known as "Captain Video," Tony was one of the first players to study

videotapes of his swing. He can remember details of every one of his 9,288 career at-bats!

It's much harder to hit .400 today than in Ted's time. More games are played at night now, and it can be harder to see the ball under the lights than in daylight.

Who's the best batter in the game today? That may be Ichiro Suzuki of the Seattle Mariners. Ichiro grew up in Japan, where he had a long and successful career for the Orix Blue Wave. By the time he left Japan in 2001 to come to the United States, he was better known than the emperor of Japan! Ichiro had no trouble adjusting to A.L. pitchers.

Ichiro Suzuki

After leading the Japan League for seven straight years, he batted .350 in 2001 to lead the A.L. No one else has ever won eight batting titles in a row.

Ichiro is a disciplined and patient hitter—he likes to wait for the pitcher to throw him a pitch he can hit. As a result, Ichiro set a Japan League record in 1997, going 216 at-bats without a strikeout.

In 2001, Ichiro racked up 242 hits, the most by a rookie since Shoeless Joe Jackson had 233 in 1911.

Shoeless Joe Jackson
Jackson put up a stunning .356 career average. But he was not allowed to play after 1920, having been caught in a gambling scandal.

No one ever played harder than Ty Cobb of the Detroit Tigers. He out-hustled everyone else. "I never could stand losing," Ty said. "Second place didn't interest me."

No kidding. When Ty retired in 1928, he had the most hits ever (4,191) and 89 other records. His .366 lifetime batting average is the highest ever.

Ty's record for hits stood until 1985, when everything came up Roses.

Ty Cobb of the Detroit Tigers

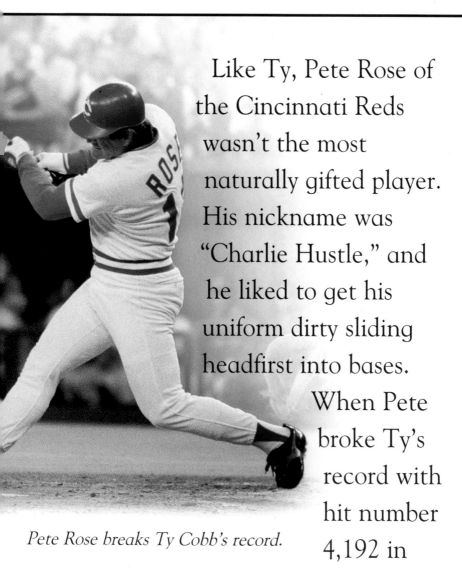

Like Ty, Pete Rose of the Cincinnati Reds wasn't the most naturally gifted player. His nickname was "Charlie Hustle," and he liked to get his uniform dirty sliding headfirst into bases.

When Pete broke Ty's record with hit number 4,192 in

Pete Rose breaks Ty Cobb's record.

1985, his son, Pete Rose II, a batboy for the Reds, ran out and gave his father a big hug on national TV. Pete retired in 1986 as the all-time leader in hits with 4,256.

While other stats get more attention than RBI, you can't win games unless you drive in runs. In 1930, Hack Wilson of the Chicago Cubs drove in 191 runs, more than anyone else in a single season before or since. Since 1938, nobody has come within 25 RBI of Hack's record.

Hack was short for a player, but very powerful. Hack smacked 56 homers in 1930. That was the N.L. record until Mark McGwire hit 70 in 1998.

Baseball's all-time RBI leader is better known as the Home Run King— Hank Aaron. "Hammerin' Hank" was more than a

Hank Aaron

power hitter, though. With 2,297 RBI for the Braves in Milwaukee and Atlanta (plus a short stint with the Brewers at the end of his career), Hank was the greatest clutch hitter ever.

Hack Wilson takes a mighty hack.

Home runs

It's going…going…gone!

The home run isn't just the most exciting play in baseball. It's the most exciting play in sports. With one swing of the bat—pow!—a slugger can jolt the fans out of their seats and change the course of a game.

Babe Ruth didn't invent the home run, but he made it famous. Before "The Bambino" came along, no one had ever hit more than 25 homers in a season. Babe rewrote the record book, bashing 60 round-trippers for the New York Yankees in 1927. That mark stood for 34 years. His career home run record (714) lasted even longer.

"The Sultan of Swat" averaged one home run for every 11.27 at-bats.

With his mighty swing, Babe Ruth changed the way the game was played.

While Babe Ruth was a powerful hitter with a big swing, Hank Aaron was smooth and steady. Hank never hit more than 47 homers in a season, but he hit 40 or more eight times.

On April 8, 1974, Hank flicked his powerful wrists and sent homer number 715 rocketing out of the park. Fans poured out of the stands and onto the field in celebration. Hank Aaron had broken Babe Ruth's record for most home runs in a career!

The chase to beat Ruth's record wasn't always fun, though. Hank received many threatening letters from people who didn't want a black man to break the record. At times, Hank admits, he was scared. But he didn't stop hitting homers until he got to 755.

Hank watches his record-setting home run fly away!

Barry watches another of his homers leave the yard.

If anyone could break Hank Aaron's home run record, it was Barry Bonds of the San Francisco Giants. Barry has already set the single-season mark. He hit an incredible 73 homers in 2001, knocking Mark McGwire, who hit 70 in 1998, out of the record books.

Barry gets better with age. His 73-homer season came when he was 37 years old. He's more than a slugger, too. In 2002, at age 38, he won his first batting title with a career-high .370 average.

Barry entered the 2003 season with 613 career homers, 47 fewer than his godfather, Willie Mays, who hit 660. So who's to say he won't break Hank's record, too? Barry, that's who. "Not that I don't think it's possible," Barry says. "I just think Hank Aaron deserves it."

Barry celebrates after another homer.

Mr. 61

While chasing Babe Ruth's record of 60 in 1961, Roger Maris got so nervous some of his hair fell out. He finished with a new record of 61 home runs.

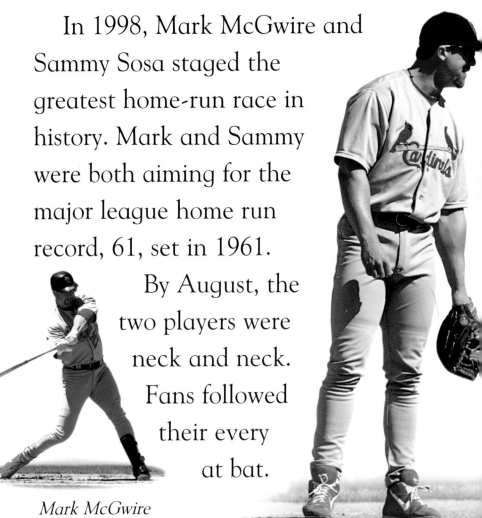

In 1998, Mark McGwire and Sammy Sosa staged the greatest home-run race in history. Mark and Sammy were both aiming for the major league home run record, 61, set in 1961.

By August, the two players were neck and neck. Fans followed their every at bat.

Mark McGwire

Sammy had blasted into the race with a record 20 homers in June. But while Sammy stayed hot all summer, Mark's pace got even hotter.

Sammy Sosa

On September 8, he smashed number 62—against Sammy's Cubs! Mark's home run rival ran in from right field to congratulate Mark. The record was finally broken, but the race was still on.

Going into the season's final weekend, Sammy went ahead 66 to 65. But Mark exploded with five homers, including two two-homer games, to finish with 70!

Home run rivals, Mark and Sammy

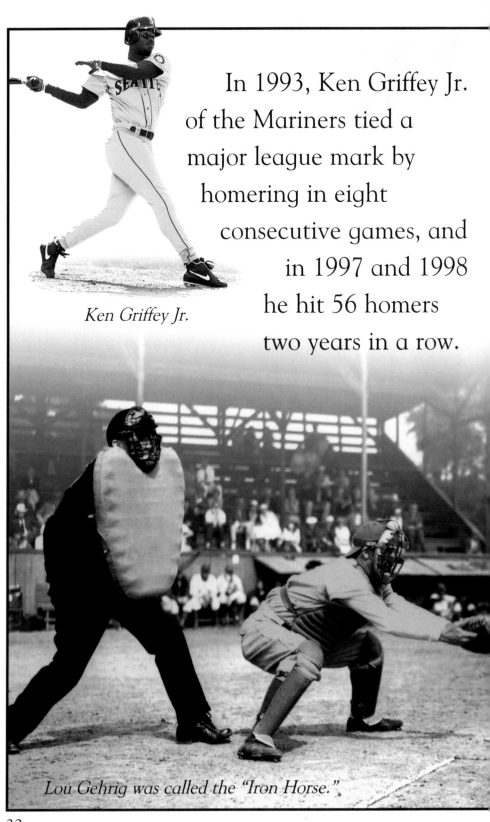

In 1993, Ken Griffey Jr. of the Mariners tied a major league mark by homering in eight consecutive games, and in 1997 and 1998 he hit 56 homers two years in a row.

Ken Griffey Jr.

Lou Gehrig was called the "Iron Horse."

Junior is a lefthanded hitter, but Mickey Mantle of the New York Yankees slugged from both sides of the plate. Mickey hit 536 homers, the most ever for a switch-hitter. He also played for seven World Series champs and hit a record 18 Series homers.

A grand slam is a home run hit with the bases loaded. It's baseball's highest-scoring play. Another famous Yankees star, Lou Gehrig, holds the record with 23 grand slams in his career.

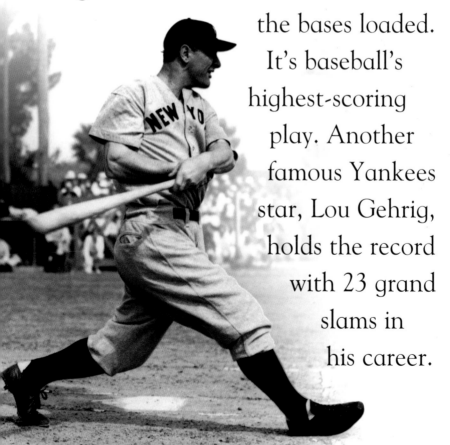

Baserunning

It is the leadoff hitter's job to get on base and make something happen—make a steal, take an extra base, and, if at all possible, score a run. Rickey Henderson was the best leadoff hitter in baseball history. In the early 1980s, Rickey earned the nickname "The Man of Steal." In 1982, Rickey set a modern-day record with 130 stolen bases.

"If my uniform doesn't get dirty, I haven't done anything in the baseball game," Rickey said.

Rickey stole at least 100 bases in a season three times, and in 1991 he blew past Lou Brock's career record of 938, holding his 939th stolen base over his head and declaring, "I am the

greatest of all time." That is hard to argue—he finished the 2002 season with 1,403 steals. Rickey also broke Babe Ruth's career record for walks, and he shattered Ty Cobb's career record for runs scored.

A scary sight for opponents: Rickey Henderson ready to run!

Ty Cobb of the Detroit Tigers was known as "The Georgia Peach." That was because of his home state, not because he was a nice guy. In fact, he was not very nice at all! Ty would do anything to win. Nobody wanted to get in his way, especially because he often sharpened the spikes on the

bottom of his shoes. When he'd slide into a base with his spikes high, infielders had to leap to get out of the way!

He would often steal second and third on the same play, and he swiped home 54 times. Ty retired in 1928 with a record 892 career steals, and he left an untold number of cuts and bruises in his wake.

Early running royalty
Mike "King" Kelly stole more than 50 bases every year from 1886 to 1890. Fans loved him. A famous song was called "Slide, Kelly, Slide!"

The Cubs haven't won the World Series since 1908. In that time, they've made many bad decisions. Their worst move may have been a trade in 1964.

Lou Brock's speed on the bases made him a superstar!

The Cubs traded outfielder Lou Brock to the St. Louis Cardinals for pitcher Ernie Broglio. Ernie won only seven more games; Lou became one of the greatest base stealers ever. Lou helped the Cardinals win two World Series, set a Series record with 14 career steals, and led the N.L. in stolen bases eight times. He smashed baseball's single-season record with 118 steals in 1974. Cubs fans are still crying about that trade!

Streaks

Baseball is a game that rewards day-in, day-out, steady play. Sticking to it, over a long period of time, equals greatness. And nothing is greater than a long hitting streak.

Pete Rose

In 1941, "Joltin' Joe" DiMaggio of the New York Yankees got a base hit in 56 games in a row. It took two sensational defensive plays by Cleveland third baseman Ken Keltner to finally stop the streak.

Joe DiMaggio had one of baseball's sweetest swings.

Joe then ran off a new 16-game streak, so if not for Ken he might have hit in 72 games in a row!

Only one player since then has approached Joe's mark. In 1978, Pete Rose, the ultimate rock-steady star, hit in 44 consecutive games. The streak captured America's attention and made worldwide headlines when it was finally stopped by the Atlanta Braves.

Cal was a Gold Glove shortstop.

Cal Ripken Jr. was the steadiest player of all. The Baltimore Orioles shortstop shattered a record no one thought could ever be broken. Lou Gehrig, the "Iron Horse," played in 2,130 consecutive games from 1925 to 1939. In 1982, Cal quietly started his own streak. Over the next 16 seasons, Cal played in 2,632 games in a row for the Baltimore Orioles.

On September 6, 1995, a sellout crowd was on hand in Baltimore.

America also watched on TV as Cal broke Lou's record. To cap off the night, Cal hit a home run to help the Orioles beat the Angels. During the streak, Cal outlasted 34 different Orioles third basemen, 26 different second basemen, and two U.S. presidents.

Cal's record streak shines on a sign in the outfield.

Casey Stengel and Mickey Mantle in Yankee Stadium.

Players strut with pride when they put on the pinstriped uniforms of the New York Yankees, and for good reason. The Yankees haven't just won a lot of World Series—they've won them in bunches.

The Yanks won three in a row from 1998 to 2000, four in a row from 1936 to 1939, and an unbroken streak of five in a row from 1949 to 1953. Manager Casey Stengel led the Yanks to Series victories over the Philadelphia Phillies, the New York Giants, and the Brooklyn Dodgers three times! Fans of other teams were frustrated because the Yankees won so much. "Break up the Yankees!" they'd yell. But it never happened. From Babe Ruth to Derek Jeter, the Yankees are often a cut above.

Famous top hat
The Yankees first played in 1903 as the New York Highlanders. They became the Yankees in 1913. Yankee Stadium opened in 1923.

All-time records

Here is a chart of some famous baseball records. Keep this list nearby as you watch Major League games....you never know when you might see a record broken!

Most career hits

• Pete Rose, 4,256

Most hits, single season

• George Sisler, 257 (1920)

Most career home runs

• Hank Aaron, 755

Most homers, single season

• Barry Bonds, 73 (2001)

Most career runs scored

• Rickey Henderson, 2,288

Most runs scored, single season

• Babe Ruth, 177 (1921)

Highest career batting average

• Ty Cobb, .367

Barry Bonds (25) gets some high fives after a homer.

Most career stolen bases
- Rickey Henderson, 1,403

Most stolen bases, single season
- Rickey Henderson, 130 (1982)

Most career strikeouts
- Nolan Ryan, 5,714

Most strikeouts, single season
- Nolan Ryan, 383 (1973)

(All totals through 2002 season.)

Glossary

American League (A.L.)
One of two groups of teams that make up the Major Leagues.

consecutive
In a row, one after the other.

control
In baseball, a pitcher's ability to throw the ball over the plate with accuracy.

Cy Young Award
Named for a famous player, this award is given every year to the top pitcher in each league.

emperor
The ceremonial leader of Japan, somewhat like a king.

Fall Classic
A nickname for the World Series, which is almost always played in October.

fan
In baseball, another word for striking out a batter.

grand slam
A home run hit with the bases loaded, scoring four runs for the batter's team.

leadoff hitter
The first player in the batting order, or the first player to bat in an inning.

National League (N.L.)
One of two groups of teams that make up the Major Leagues.

RBI
Short for runs batted in, a statistic that counts the number of runs scored that result from a batter's performance at the plate.

shutout
When a pitcher throws a complete game and doesn't allow any runs.

spikes
Short blades of metal on the bottom of baseball shoes that help players dig into the dirt.

trade
In pro sports, teams can send their players to other teams in exchange for players or money.

Triple Crown
An unofficial award given to a hitter who leads his league in homers, RBI, and batting average for a season.